# SENSING GOD?
# RECONSIDERING THE
# PATRISTIC DOCTRINE OF
# "SPIRITUAL SENSATION"
# FOR CONTEMPORARY
# THEOLOGY AND ETHICS

THE PÈRE MARQUETTE
LECTURE IN THEOLOGY
2022

# SENSING GOD? RECONSIDERING THE PATRISTIC DOCTRINE OF "SPIRITUAL SENSATION" FOR CONTEMPORARY THEOLOGY AND ETHICS

by

SARAH COAKLEY

MARQUETTE
UNIVERSITY
PRESS

Library of Congress Cataloging-in-Publication Data

Names: Coakley, Sarah, 1951- author.
Title: Sensing God? : reconsidering the patristic doctrine of "spiritual sensation" for contemporary theology and ethics / by Sarah Coakley.
Description: Milwaukee, Wisconsin : Marquette University Press, [2022] |
  Series: The Père Marquette lecture in theology ; 2022 |
  Includes bibliographical references. | Summary: "This study provides a new critical assessment of Jean Daniélou's classic rendition of the theme of "spiritual sensation" in the work of Gregory of Nyssa, arguing that it has surprising wider relevance for such pressing contemporary cultural problems as racism, sexism and addiction to pornography"--Provided by publisher.
Identifiers: LCCN 2022026083 | ISBN 9781626005143 (hardcover)
Subjects: LCSH: Daniélou, Jean. Platonisme et théologie mystique. |
  Gregory, of Nyssa, Saint, approximately 335-approximately 394. |
  Mysticism--History--Early church, ca. 30-600. | Senses and sensation--Religious aspects--Christianity. | Spirituality--Christianity. | Knowledge, Theory of (Religion) | Fathers of the church. | Christian literature, Early--Greek authors--History and criticism.
Classification: LCC BR65.G76 D3325 2022 | DDC 270.2--dc23/eng/20220804
LC record available at https://lccn.loc.gov/2022026083

ASSOCIATION
of UNIVERSITY
PRESSES

Marquette University Press
MILWAUKEE

## FOREWORD

The 2022 Père Marquette Lecture in Theology is the fifty-second in a series commemorating the missions and explorations of Père Jacques Marquette, SJ (1637–75). This series of lectures was begun in 1969 under the auspices of the Marquette University Department of Theology. The Joseph A. Auchter Family Endowment Fund had endowed the lecture series. Joseph Auchter (1894–1986), a native of Milwaukee, was a banking and paper industry executive and a long-time supporter of education. The fund was established by his children as a memorial to him.

## SARAH COAKLEY

*Photo by John Cairns*

Sarah Coakley previously held the Norris-Hulse Professorship at Cambridge University from 2007 to 2018. From 2018 she has been an Honorary

Professor at the Logos Institute, St Andrews University, and from 2019 a Visiting Professorial Fellow at the Australian Catholic University (Melbourne and Rome); she is recently retired. Professor Coakley is an Honorary Fellow of Oriel College, Oxford, an Emeritus Fellow of Murray Edwards College, Cambridge, a Fellow of the British Academy, and a member of the European Academy of Arts and Sciences. She holds honorary degrees from the Universities of Lund, St Andrews, Toronto (St Michael's College), and London (Heythrop College).

Born in London in 1951, Sarah Coakley was educated at Cambridge (BA/MA, PhD) and Harvard (Th.M) Universities. She held earlier academic positions at Lancaster University (1976–1991), Oriel College, Oxford (1991–93), Harvard Divinity School (1993–2007; Mallinckrodt Professor, 1995–2007), and a visiting Professorship at Princeton University (2003–4). She gave the Gifford Lectures at the University of Aberdeen in 2012.

She is the author or co-editor of nearly two-dozen books, including *Powers and Submissions: Philosophy, Spirituality and Gender* (Oxford, Blackwell, 2002); (ed.), *Re-Thinking Gregory of Nyssa* (Oxford, Blackwell, 2003); (coed.) *The Spiritual Senses: Perceiving God in Western Spirituality* (Cambridge, C.U.P., 2012); *God, Sexuality and the Self: An Essay 'On the Trinity'* (Cambridge, C.U.P., 2013); and *The New Asceticism: Sexuality, Gender and the Quest for God* (London, Bloomsbury, 2016).

Her forthcoming publications include: *The Vowed Life: The Promise of Discipleship*, co-edited with Matthew Bullimore (Norwich, Canterbury Press, 2022); *The Oxford Handbook of the Reception of Christian Theology*, co-edited with Richard Cross and Jonathan Teubner (Oxford, O.U.P., 2023); *Sacrifice: Defunct or Desired? A New Religious and Theological Analysis* (The Richard Lectures, UVA) (Charlottesville, VA, U.V.A Press, 2023); and *Sin, Racism and Divine Darkness: An Essay 'On Human Nature'* (Cambridge, C.U.P., 2024) (vol. 2 of Coakley's 4-vol. systematic theology).

Dr. Coakley is currently engaged in writing the remaining volumes of her systematic theology and editing her recent papers in philosophy of religion.

# SENSING GOD? RECONSIDERING THE PATRISTIC DOCTRINE OF 'SPIRITUAL SENSATION' FOR CONTEMPORARY THEOLOGY AND ETHICS

## SARAH COAKLEY

### INTRODUCTION: WHY THE RECOVERY OF THE 'SPIRITUAL SENSES' TRADITION TODAY?

This lecture is concerned with the tradition of 'spiritual sensation', so-called, in the early Greek Fathers; and, in its first section, I engage with the issue of how this almost-lost, and somewhat arcane, patristic tradition of theological epistemology suddenly became repristinated in the work of a group of extraordinarily gifted younger Jesuits in the inter-war years in Europe, all of whom were to have illustrious and controversial ecclesiastical careers thereafter.

Despite what were later to become important, even painful, divergences in their individual approaches and theological emphases, the young Karl Rahner, Hans Urs von Balthasar and Jean Daniélou (the latter two significantly tutored together by their slightly-older confrère, Henri de Lubac, at the Jesuit house at Fourvière in Lyon in the early 1930s), all played key roles in this repristination.[1] And while the recovery of the patristic 'spiritual sensation' tradition was not at that time explicitly lifted up by them, or indeed others, as their most important or emblematic theological contribution (for they were too busy fretting, in their *different* ways, against the mandatory neo-scholastic Thomist synthesis of their day), we can now see in retrospect that this theme was a surprisingly unifying thread guiding the efforts of them all at so-called *ressourcement* (the recovery of earlier Christian tradition for today's theological and spiritual needs).

---

1 Earlier reflections on dimensions of this story may be found in eds. Paul L. Gavrilyuk and Sarah Coakley, *The Spiritual Senses: Perceiving God in Western Christianity* (Cambridge, C.U.P., 2012), esp. ch. 1 (Mark J. McInroy, 'Origen of Alexandria'), ch. 2 (Sarah Coakley, 'Gregory of Nyssa') and ch. 15 (Mark J. McInroy, 'Karl Rahner and Hans Urs von Balthasar'). As will be clear in what follows, in the years since the publication of this book I have revised and nuanced some of my earlier views expressed there in my chapter on Nyssen.

That is, for each one of them, the recovery of the Eastern patristic world of thought and spirituality was an energizing and reforming resistance to the then-dominant form of Roman neo-Thomistic scholasticism; and it was so in an important and serendipitous way also—I am going to argue further—because of its natural spiritual resonances with the required *Ignatian* formation through which they were all passing as Jesuits. But this was only the beginning of a new, contemporary, story about 'spiritual sensation' which I want to suggest is still unfolding today, and moves well outside their earlier purview, for all its seminal significance. To that I shall come at the end of this presentation.

My lecture, then, will proceed in three dialectically-related stages. In the first section I shall recall just some of the details of this Jesuit recovery of the 'spiritual sense' tradition in the early 1930s and onwards, in order to set the stage for the rest of the lecture. In the second section I shall turn specifically to the significance of this particular thematic in the thought of the fourth-century Cappadocian Father, Gregory of Nyssa, since I want to suggest that he had a very *distinctive* rendition of its importance, and one of immense continuing significance, even now. It was Jean Daniélou who first drew extended attention to this topic of 'spiritual sense' in Gregory of Nyssa in his famous monograph of 1944, *Platonisme et théologie mystique* (which had earlier formed his doctoral thesis)[2]. But I have argued of late[3]—and shall again here, though with some new modifications of that earlier analysis—that Daniélou did not really get to the bottom of the importance of this topic as it manifested itself *throughout* Nyssen's career; and that its challenge and interest is wider than is normally presumed. It was not, that is, merely a 'mystical' doctrine for those well-advanced in contemplative practice, as Daniélou seemed to suppose in his early work, but a whole theory of the progressive sanctification and purification of the sensual realm—one intended for all the baptized, and even perhaps beyond them in the 'pagan' world (to judge from occasional passages in Gregory of Nyssa's own *oeuvre*).[4] In short, it is a distinctive philosophical and moral *epistemology* that Nyssen offers us here, one in which body and soul are progressively united and transformed, even by working *on* and *with* the 'flesh'. This teaching remains frustratingly unsystematic in Gregory's presentation, to be sure (and hence

---

2   Jean Daniélou, *Platonisme et thélogie mystique: Essai sur la doctrine spirituelle de saint Grégoire de Nysse* (Paris, Aubier, 1944; 2nd edit., 1954). It remains surprising that this extraordinarily creative and important monograph has never been translated into English or other languages.

3   Sarah Coakley, 'Gregory of Nyssa', in *The Spiritual Senses*, ch. 2, 36–55.

4   See the discussion, below, section II, of Nyssen's *De anima et resurrectione*, in particular.

the difficulty of interpreting it accurately); but it is full of interest and promise not only for contemporary *theological* repristinations of the same topic, but also evocative for what I now see as some of the more creative and daring strands of secular analytic *epistemology* today (specifically for the realms of 'virtue' and 'vice' epistemology, so-called, and for analyses of 'epistemic injustice', 'perceptual distortion', and sexist and racist 'prejudice', as these topics relate to important contemporary moral issues)[5].

In the third section of this lecture, then, I shall turn explicitly to this contemporary philosophical realm, and muse prospectively on what a developed theory of Christian 'spiritual sensation' along the lines suggested by Nyssen could mean for critical

---

5 Analytic philosophy has in recent decades remarkably broadened its earlier epistemological focus on the conditions of 'scientific' knowledge, bequeathed from the Enlightenment, and often now reduced to the problem of reliably (re)identifying 'medium-sized dry goods' (J. L. Austin) at a distance of several paces. The turn to the examination of the *moral* dimensions of knowledge ('virtue' and 'vice' epistemology), and the extension of creative earlier feminist epistemologies to examinations of racism, prejudicial perceptual distortion, and testimonial injustice, are exciting features of contemporary epistemology in which women philosophers have played particularly important roles. See Section III, below, and (for a general introduction to virtue epistemology), J. Turri, 'Virtue Epistemology', https://plato.stanford.edu/entries/epistemology-virtue/ (accessed March 28, 2022, last updated October 2021).

engagement as contemporary religious practitioners
with this burgeoning secular philosophical literature, and with some of the deepest spiritual and
moral *aporiai* of our day: 'systemic' racism (as it is
now called);[6] still-unacknowledged but pervasive
societal sexism;[7] and the corrupting and addic-
tive features of online pornography.[8] We may, of
course, not even yet be accustomed to thinking
of these problems as connected at all, let alone as

---

6  What 'systemic' means in this context is a continuing matter for debate. In the last section of this lecture I discuss the
   problem of how potentially empirically-identifiable forms
   of racism (in the legal, economic, educational and political
   realms) vie with appeals to inchoate and unconscious forms
   of prejudice ('implicit bias') which are notoriously hard to
   quantify or assess.

7  In recent years the *Me Too* movement has drawn urgent
   attention to the ways in which modern Western feminism
   has yet to achieve its basic goal to overcome manifest challenges to women's flourishing in the forms of sexual violence and harassment: see https://en.wikipedia.org/wiki/
   MeToo_movement (accessed March 30, 2022).

8  Bernadette Barton, *The Pornification of America: How
   Raunch Culture is Ruining our Society* (New York, New York
   University Press, 2021) is one recent analysis and exposé
   of the way in which pornographic images are now culturally pervasive in the United States, and the implications of
   this phenomenon for women's lives. Far from advocating
   religious sexual conservatism in *riposte*, however, Barton
   argues that 'raunch culture' and repressive religious control
   of women are simply 'two sides of the same coin'.

manifestations of an underlying *epistemological* malaise (and please be aware that I am not of course claiming that modern pornography originally *produced* historic forms of racism and sexism). But if it is a sinful and habitual corruption of the *sensorium* that unites these phenomena at some deep level, then we are necessarily drawn to reflect, in contrast, on what might heal and redirect our sensual lives more generally, and how that question relates to the very life and responsibilities of the Church in our society to think afresh about these problems.

That is all by way of anticipation of what will follow.

But before I plunge into the three main sections of this lecture, let me essay a preliminary working definition of 'spiritual sensation', a notion which is by no means univocally understood even by those who have utilized it intentionally in the Christian tradition.[9]

---

9 See Paul L. Gavrilyuk and Sarah Coakley, 'Introduction' to eds. Gavrilyuk and Coakley, *The Spiritual Senses*, 1–19, which discusses the varied history and uses of the term 'spiritual sensation', and the paradoxical fact that some who can credibly be said to be exponents of this tradition do not even regularly use the *term* itself. For an important earlier dictionary treatment of 'spiritual sense' in the patristic period which greatly assisted the editors of *The Spiritual Senses*, see Mariette Canévet, 'Sens spirituels', in *Dictionnaire de spiritualité*, vol. XIV (Paris, Beauchesne, 1990), 598–617. For a contemporary French phenomenological account of

A definition I would propose, therefore, at least as a starting point, is this: *A theory of 'spiritual sensation' represents an approach to human sensual, perceptual, and accompanying moral capacities as labile and malleable, according to their congruence with the graced and purifying work of God, the Holy Spirit.*

The crucial proposed insight here, note, is that even our ordinary human perceptions or sensations of the world are not simply available to us on a universally-given epistemic 'flat-plane', so to speak, but are subject to certain transformations, both negative and positive, according—on the one hand—to spiritual transitions in the realm of sanctification, but also—on the other—to factors of habit, training, manipulation or even corruption. That is why the sensual and the ethical are so closely entangled in this approach.

To be frank, we are dealing here with a set of epistemological presumptions that became, for the most part, quite alien to *modern* 'secular' philosophy in the era of Enlightenment, and are only now being recovered (as I have already suggested), in secularized forms, in varieties of 'alternative' contemporary epistemology. Moreover, let us be clear that these presumptions were also not universally shared, either, by Christian patristic and

---

the body which is greatly indebted to Daniélou's patristic work on 'spiritual sense', see Jean-Louis Chrétien, *Symbolique du Corps: La tradition chrétienne du Cantique des Cantiques* (Paris, Universitaires de France, 2005).

scholastic philosophers and theologians in general.
(It is, for instance, a moot point whether Thomas
Aquinas has any hint of such a doctrine in his own
magisterial—broadly Aristotelian—epistemological armoury[10]). More often, in fact, it was theologians of a 'contemplative' or 'mystical' *Tendenz*,
especially those standing in the tradition of Origen of Alexandria, or of those whom he influenced
directly or indirectly, that this teaching arose; and
it was also regularly correlated, in the patristic
and medieval eras, with a particular approach to
reading Scripture allegorically (also in *its* 'spiritual
sense', so-called, as opposed to its 'literal sense').[11]
For thus it was taught—as in Origen—that a life-
time's perusal of the Scriptures would in due time,
under the impress of the Spirit, lead potentially to
a final and full union with Christ himself, in whom
all sensual and psychic life is renewed.

---

10 See Richard Cross's discussion of this issue in 'Thomas
Aquinas', eds. Gavrilyuk and Coakley, *The Spiritual Senses*,
174–189, in which he denies that Aquinas has any need for
a doctrine of 'spiritual sense' in his own epistemology. An
in-depth analysis of Aquinas's doctrine of the Holy Spirit
in *Summa Theologiae*, III, might however reveal that Aquinas presents something akin to the teaching through that
doctrinal medium.

11 See Henri de Lubac, *Histoire et ésprit: l'intelligence de l'écriture
d'après Origène* (Paris, Montaigne, 1950,) tr. Anne Englund
Nash, *History and Spirit: The Understanding of Scripture
According to Origen* (San Francisco, Ignatius Books, 2007).

So much by way of introduction. I turn now to our first major section of the lecture, and to the remarkable company of Jesuits who unexpectedly re-converged on our topic of 'spiritual sensation' in the 1930s and 1940s in Europe.

## I. A JESUIT RECUPERATION: FROM IGNATIAN SPIRITUAL DISCERNMENT BACK TO PATRISTIC EPISTEMOLOGY?

In 1932, the same year he was ordained after his theologate in the Netherlands, the young German Jesuit Karl Rahner published an extraordinary first article in the French journal *Revue d'ascétique et de mystique* (originally hand-written, apparently, in a little exercise book in honour of his father; it later also came out in another, slightly shorter, version in German).[12] It was a study of the 'beginnings of the doctrine of spiritual sense in Origen'; and the second part of the undertaking appeared the following year

---

12  Karl Rahner, 'Le début d'une doctrine des cinq sens spiri-
    tuels chez Origène', *Revue d'ascétique et mystique* 13 (1932),
    113–45; the German version was newly edited and slightly
    shortened as 'Die "geistlichen Sinne" nach Origenes', in
    *Schriften zur Theologie*, vol. XII: *Theologie ·aud Erfahrung
    des Geistes*, ed. K. Neufeld (Zürich, Benziger Verlag,
    1975), 111–136. The English translation of the German
    is by David Morland, OSB in *Theological Investigations*,
    vol. XVI: *Experience of the Spirit: Source of Theology* (New
    York, Seabury Press, 1979), 81–103.

in the same French journal—an equally important discussion of the developing importance of the same doctrine in the medieval West, and especially in Bonaventure (whose thoughts on 'spiritual touch' were, in turn, significantly to influence Ignatius of Loyola later).[13] It is obvious from the first of these articles, however, that Rahner's interest (and his slightly wooden categories of analysis as applied to Origen, which will be mentioned again later[14]) arose out of the hugely-influential recent treatment of 'spiritual sense' in another, and rather different, context. That was that of a French Jesuit of a slightly older generation, Fr. Augustin Poulain (1836–1919), whose controversial assessment of the *Carmelite*

---

13 Karl Rahner, 'La doctrine des "sens spirituels" au Moyen-Âge, en particulier chez saint Bonoventure', *Revue d'ascétique et mystique* 14 (1933), 263–99, English translation also in *Theological Investigations*, vol. XVI, 104–134.

14 See Mark McInroy's discussion of this problem in his chapter, 'Origen of Alexandria', eds. Gavrilyuk and Coakley, *The Spiritual Senses*, 20–35: there is not only in Rahner's treatment the *a priori* insistence that all five senses must be involved, but a certain obsession with whether Origen's discussion of 'sense' is 'metaphorical' or 'analogical' (a distinction important for anyone trained in the Thomistic tradition, of course, but alien to the context of Origen). As McInroy shows, this issue has continued to haunt secondary discussion of the issue since, and is arguably quite distracting in trying to grasp Origen's more subtle forms of communication to different constituents and in different contexts.

tradition of 'spirituality' and its stages of ascent, expressed in his influential volume *The Graces of Interior Prayer*, was originally published in 1901, but eventually ran into multiple editions in several languages.[15] Poulain's critical, and frankly rather curious, re-interpretation of John of the Cross, which animated the volume,[16] did however involve a whole chapter devoted to 'spiritual sensation';[17]

---

15 *Des grâces d'oraison* (Paris, Beauchesne, 1901), was published to great acclaim and controversy, ran into nine editions during the author's lifetime, and two others later. The English translation, from the 6th edition, is by Leonora L. Yorke Smith: *The Graces of Interior Prayer* (London, Kegan Paul, Trench, Trübner, 1910).

16 One of the most trenchant criticisms of Poulain's understandings of the stages of 'mystical ascent' according to John of the Cross (especially in regard to what Poulain called the 'ligature' between 'meditation' and 'contemplation') may be found in the celebrated spiritual teaching of John Chapman, OSB, *Spiritual Letters* (London, Burns and Oates, 1935). I discuss this particular point in my own *Powers and Submissions: Spirituality, Philosophy and Gender* (Oxford, Blackwell, 2002), esp. 42–3.

17 Poulain, *The Graces of Interior Prayer*, ch. VI, 88–113. This chapter consists first of a distinctive (and indeed controversial) interpretation of the meaning of 'spiritual sense' as relating to 'mystic union' and how it is 'felt'; and that is followed by a selection of 'extracts' supposedly supporting Poulain's thesis. Only one of these texts comes from the patristic period (from Augustine's *Confessions*); most are considerably later.

and this was the theme whose much deeper historical roots and meaning Rahner now discerningly
sought to expose. What Rahner perhaps implicitly
perceived was that what in the modern period had
become solely a category for use in *spiritual direction* and *spiritual discernment* (as kept alive particularly in the Jesuit tradition by Fr. Giovanni Battista
Scaramelli in the 18th century,[18] and then actively
revived by Poulain), actually had an original force
in the Greek patristic author Origen which was
more generally *epistemological* in relation to the
whole Christian life. Indeed, what was involved in
Origen was a line of approach—as we have already
suggested—almost completely lost in Enlightenment and post-Enlightenment *philosophical* epistemology, guided as that was by the new desire to
attain a universal 'scientific' status of certainty in
empirical investigations of the outside world.[19] In

---

18 See Giovanni Battista Scaramelli, *Il direttorio mistico, ind-
irizzatto a' direttori di quelle anime, che iddio conduce per la
via della contemplazione* (Venice, S. Occhi, 1754); partial
English translation, by D. H. S. Nicholson, as *A Handbook
of Mystical Theology: Being an Abridgement of Il direttorio
mistico* (London, John M. Watkins, 1913).

19 Susan E. Shreiner traces this modern urge to 'certainty'
back to the Reformation era, in her remarkable book, *Are
You Alone Wise? The Search for Certainty in the Early Modern Era* (Oxford, O.U.P., 2011), in which we begin to see
the divergence between 'religious' or 'experiential' certainty
(as in Teresa of Ávilla, *par excellence*), and the burgeoning

Origen, in contrast, the idea was that the individual development of our five senses towards refinement and sensitivity to *Christ* might be a life-time's undertaking, a project indeed coterminous with sanctification itself, and therefore one in which individual Christians would inevitably find themselves on different levels of development in the journey at different times.[20] Such a revolutionary, but almost forgotten, notion was also, then, a very different perception again of the importance of 'spiritual sense' than that associated with the very particular meditative technique of the 'application of the senses' in Ignatius's *Spiritual Exercises*, Second Week,[21]

---

'scientific' certainty of the Cartesian 'turn'. For the latter, and its background in modern French philosophical scepticism, see Michael J. Buckley, *At the Origins of Modern Atheism* (New Haven, Yale U.P., 1987).

20  A particularly insightful rendition of this progressivist theme in Origen is to be found in Judith Kovacs, 'Servant of Christ and Steward of the Mysteries of God: the Purpose of the Pauline Letter according to Origen's *Homilies on 1 Corinthians*', in eds. Paul M. Blowers, Angela Russell Christman, David Hunter and Robin Darling Young, *In Dominico Eloquio: Essays on Patristic Exegesis in Honor of Robert Louis Wilken* (Grand Rapids, MI, Eerdmans, 2002), 147–71.

21  See Ignatius of Loyola, *The Spiritual Exercises of St Ignatius of Loyola*, tr. Thomas Corbishley (Wheathampstead, Anthony Clarke, 1963), Second Week, Fifth Contemplation, 'An Application of the Five Senses to the First and Second Contemplation', 48–51. Here Ignatius describes

something with which all the Jesuits in this narrative were of course well familiar. The interesting new detective story for Rahner, however, was where that (distinctively Ignatian) practice had its ultimate origins, and how it related to this patristic fundament.

Now, while Rahner was enjoying his first success with an academic publication in a French journal, the young Swiss Jesuit Hans Urs von Balthasar was just about to arrive in Lyon (in 1933) to start his own theological training at Fourvière, and from the next year to sit regularly at the feet of his slightly-older colleague, Henri de Lubac, along with a few other gifted French Jesuit students later to become celebrated. As von Balthasar writes autobiographically of his time at Fourvière, 'While all the others went off to play football, Daniélou, Bouillard and I and a few others . . . got down to Origen, Gregory of Nyssa, and Maximus. I [later] wrote a book on each of these' (he adds

---

how profit will be gained from the . . . imaginative use of the five senses' in contemplation. Timothy O'Brien, SJ, has recently argued, however, that it is Ignatius's *Autobiography* and *Spiritual Diary* that are more important for understanding Ignatius's own distinctive understanding of 'spiritual sense', than these strands in his *Exercises*: see O'Brien, Timothy W., 'Con Ojos Interiores: Ignatius of Loyola and the Spiritual Senses', *Studies in Spirituality* 26 (2016), 263–281.

laconically).[22] Daniélou was of course to publish *his* important monograph on Gregory of Nyssa ten years later; and this little Greek-reading group also proved to be at the origins of the great *Sources Chrétiennes* publishing series, which soon was to bring the Fathers afresh to the general-reading French public in accessible paperback editions.[23] It cannot be a coincidence, moreover, that the three Greek fathers who were first and specially chosen by de Lubac for focused reading (Origen, Nyssen,

---

22  Peter Henrici, 'A Sketch of Balthasar's Life', in ed. David L. Schindler, *Hans Urs Von Balthasar: His Life and Work* (San Francisco, Ignatius Press, 1991), 7–43, at p. 11. The opening section of von Balthasar's monograph on Gregory of Nyssa is also *à propos*: see his *Presence and Thought: An Essay on the Religious Philosophy of Gregory of Nyssa* (orig. 1939/1942, translated Marc Sebanc, San Francisco, Ignatius Press, 1995), 12–13: here Balthasar promises that his study of Nyssen will be accompanied by monographs on Origen and Maximus Confessor. For these, see: *Origen, Spirit and Fire: A Thematic Anthology of His Writings* (orig. 1938/1956, translated Robert J. Daly, SJ, Washington, DC, Catholic University of America Press, 1984); and *Cosmic Liturgy: The Universe According to Maximus the Confessor* (3rd. edit., 1988, translated Brian E. Daley, SJ, San Francisco, Ignatius Press, 2003).

23  The first publication of this new series came out in the midst of WWII, in 1942, and this was, significantly, an edition of Gregory of Nyssa's *Life of Moses*. From the start an editorial decision was made not to restrict texts to those which were officially 'orthodox'. See https://en.wikipedia.org/wiki/Sources_Chrétiennes (accessed on March 29, 2022).

Maximus, all slightly under a cloud of historical suspicion for different reasons[24]), *all* propounded their
own theories of 'spiritual sense', founded in Origen's
original insights, though with variations; and all
three of these Greek authors adhered to some version of the Platonic/'erotic' notion of the fundamental human longing for God which was to become so
important and controversial in de Lubac's own rein-
terpretation of Thomas's idea of the 'natural desire
[*desiderium*]' for God.[25] Moreover, de Lubac was
later (in 1950) to publish his own celebrated discussion of the 'spiritual sense' of *Scripture* in Origen,[26]

---

24  Origen had remained suspect because of the 'Origenist controversy' and the suspicions thereby in relation to his 'orthodoxy',
Nyssen for his universalism and questionably orthodox Christology, and Maximus (albeit vindicated at the third council of
Constantinople, 680–81), for his distinctive views on Christ's
two wills and his wider cosmological speculations.

25  For this theme in Aquinas and de Lubac's distinctive rendition of its importance, two relevant recent publications are:
Stephen Wang, 'Aquinas on Human Happiness and the
Natural Desire for God', *New Blackfriars* 88 (2007), 322–
324, and Nicholas J. Healy, 'Henri de Lubac on Nature and
Grace: Some Recent Contributions to the Debate', *Commu-
nio: International Catholic Review* 35 (2008), 535–564.

26  See n. 11, above, and—for a recent assessment of this
important strand in de Lubac's thinking, Kevin L. Hughes,
'The Spiritual Interpretation of Scripture', in ed. Jordan
Hillebert, *T & T Clark Companion to Henri de Lubac*
(London, Bloomsbury, 2017), 205–223.

a topic (as already mentioned above) correlated to Origen's epistemological meaning of 'spiritual sense', and by which de Lubac attempted to restore the ancient allegorical method of exegesis—and thereby the quest for Christ throughout the Scriptural corpus—to central spiritual consideration for the Western Church's life and liturgy.

In short, we can say of this inconspicuous little Greek-reading group at Fourvière that perhaps never had an afternoon's alternative to football had such significant ecclesiastical aftershocks, which we are—I suggest—still even now assimilating.

But I hope I have said enough in this first section of my lecture to indicate already how exciting and novel were the developments in the understanding of the neglected Greek patristic and Latin medieval doctrine of 'spiritual sense' in these crucial inter-war years in Jesuit houses in Europe.

But what, we might enquire, was really at stake here *theologically*? Why did it matter, at this particular juncture of modern theological history, that an apparently obscure pre-modern theory of religious cognition and sensation suddenly attracted the attention of young scholars bent on reforming the Church via the recuperation of Greek patristic sources? The question becomes the more pointed, of course, because the younger Jesuits who converged briefly in their study of this topic, in particular Rahner and von Balthasar, were later to *divide* most contentiously in important theoretic and theological ways on questions of religious epistemology and revelatory authority (the one, Rahner, under the influence of Heidegger, the other, von Balthasar under the very different influence of Barth[27]). On this particular point, Stephen Fields, SJ has thrown important light on how von Balthasar's and Rahner's *different* renditions of Bonaventure on 'spiritual sense' already seem to mark that divergence, suggesting that Rahner's early rendition of Bonaventure perhaps foreshadows his famous Heideggerian idea of the supposed natural human *Vorgriff* ('pre-apprehension') in relation to God.[28]

Yet in subtle contrast to this analysis by Fields (though not in rejection of his proposal about the differing understandings of Bonaventure in the two men), Mark McInroy has suggested in response that, if we take the importance of the re-discovery

---

27　This is how the disjunction between Rahner and von Balthasar is often understood, and it is not without overall truth; however, a discerning reading of Balthasar will also show his own indebtedness to Heidegger at various points: see, most recently, Mark J. McInroy, 'Manifesting Being: Hans Urs von Balthasar's Interpretation of Bonaventure and the Transcendental Status of Beauty', in ed. Alice Ramos, *Beauty and the Good: Past Interpretations and their Contemporary Relevance* (Washington, D.C., Catholic University of America Press, 2020), 269–287.

28　Stephen Fields, SJ, 'Balthasar and Rahner on the Spiritual Senses', *Theological Studies* 57 (1996), 224–41.

of patristic and medieval 'spiritual sensation' to *both* of these titans at the start of their theological careers as seriously as we should, then it may be that we can see their subsequent divergence and enmity as *less* marked than heretofore. As McInroy puts it, 'If Rahner's understanding of spiritual touch [*sc.* in the early 1930s] [already] comes to significantly shape his understanding of the point of contact between the human being and God, then the concerns about Rahner's anthropology being overly dictated by his *philosophical* starting point will need to be reconsidered';[29] whereas, conversely, once we fully understand the role that the (epistemological) spiritual senses explicitly play in Balthasar's theological aesthetic throughout his career—as McInroy has himself shown in an important monograph[30]—then we see that there is, after all, an 'anthropological structure' undergirding his revelatory theological conception of the 'form' of God.[31] In both men's thinking, then, the

---

29  Mark J. McInroy, 'Karl Rahner and Hans Urs von Balthasar', in eds. Gavrilyuk and Coakley, *The Spiritual Senses*, 273–4, my emphasis.

30  Mark J. McInroy, *Balthasar on the Spiritual Senses: Perceiving Splendour* (Oxford, O.U.P., 2014).

31  Mark J. McInroy, 'Karl Rahner and Hans Urs von Balthasar', 274. For a further important reassessment of the relation of Rahner's and von Balthasar's systematic projects, see Jennifer Newsome Martin, 'Balthasar and Rahner', in *The Oxford Handbook of Hans Urs von Balthasar* (forthcoming).

continuing importance of the 'spiritual sense' tradition arguably endured, despite Rahner's rather unexpected failure to mention it again explicitly after his early notable publishing success with the theme.

Yet, to sum up now the lessons of this opening discussion: the 'spiritual senses' tradition came to be significant once more at this creative, and crucial, inter-War period of Catholic thinking for a number of reasons which we do well to carry forward from here into the rest of this lecture. First, it gave access to a forgotten strand of patristic thought which could re-open the possibility of a profound integration of Scriptural meditation, theology, and personal prayer, and so re-enliven a theological scenario dominated, for Roman Catholics at the time, by the seemingly arid teaching of the neo-Scholastic textbooks. Moreover, as fascinating recent historical research by Sarah Shortall has shown, such a theological push-back by these Jesuits was also one with important *political* evocations in the French (Third Republic) governmental context of the day, where issues of top-down authority, and the mandated separation of church and state, were equally being tested and re-negotiated.[32]

---

32 See Sarah Shortall, *Soldiers of God in a Secular World: Catholic Theology and Twentieth Century French Politics* (Cambridge, MA, Harvard University Press, 2021), a fascinating study of the enforced separation of church and state in early 20th century France, and the different roles

Secondly, the 'spiritual senses' teaching also represented a way in which the distinctively early-modern
Ignatian tradition of spiritual practice maintained
by the Jesuits could be traced back into its remoter
patristic and medieval roots and influences, and
brought into some suggestive congruence thereby
with a much older, Platonic-Christian, understanding of a fundamental religious 'desire' in the human in
which intellectual, affective and aesthetic responses
were fully united. This was a correlated, 'spiritual',
way in which the neo-Thomist system itself could be
re-thought and re-enlivened, not only by the affectiv-
ity of the Ignatian tradition itself, but by engagement
with its deeper genealogical roots in the East.[33]

------

of Jesuit and Dominican theologians (both communities
expelled from France in 1880) in reconsidering the relation
of the neo-Thomist 'natural' and 'supernatural' distinction
in response to this political crisis. In this light, the blended
'naturalism'/'supernaturalism' of the Eastern patristic 'spiritual sense' tradition, which so attracted the various Jesuits
discussed in this lecture, had an implicit political, as well as
theological, significance.

33  In Rahner, as we have already seen, there was a genealogical
desire to explain the link from Origen's 'spiritual sensation'
teaching to the much later spiritual theory and practices of
Ignatius of Loyola. In Daniélou, as we shall now discuss in
section II, the deeper interest is in 'mysticism', so-called, and
the thematic links between 'spiritual sensation' in Gregory
of Nyssa and John of the Cross. Von Balthasar's various
later discussions of spiritual sense (which drew on a variety

Thirdly, therefore, and despite the acknowledged *variety* of different strands in the wider Christian 'spiritual sense' tradition, it also represented an exciting apologetic and *philosophical* resource; for it had the potential, at least, to provide an account of a responsive anthropological fulcrum from which to combat sceptical modern questions about the very possibility of belief in God itself. And de Lubac, Rahner, and von Balthasar were all to develop quite different apologetic strategies which plausibly can be traced back to this early inspiration.[34] Such, then, were the wide-ranging theological concerns of the day which all found exciting resonance in the rediscovery of the 'spiritual senses' teaching.

---

of authors, both East and West) were to lead to a particular understanding of how the 'form' of God could be responded to aesthetically: see again Mark J, McInroy, *Balthasar on the Spiritual Senses*, especially chs. 1, 2, 4 and 5.

34  For the neglected importance of 'natural theology' in de Lubac (in a fresh and original key of his own, including the appeal to an Origenistic 'spiritual sense') see Philip Moller, SJ, 'Henri de Lubac and the Knowledge of God: Natural Theology and the Crisis of *la nouvelle théologie*' (PhD dissertation, Cambridge, 2019, now revised and forthcoming). For a comparison of Rahner's and von Balthasar's 'foundational' or 'natural' theologies, also beholden in seminal ways to the 'spiritual sense' tradition, see again nn. 29 and 31, above.

## II. GREGORY OF NYSSA (C. 335–C.395) ON 'SPIRITUAL SENSATION': A REASSESSMENT AND REAPPLICATION

But what now of Rahner's and von Balthasar's confrère Jean Daniélou, also a pupil of de Lubac,[35] for
whom Gregory of Nyssa, rather than Origen, became
the focus of his doctoral work? How were Daniélou's
intellectual and spiritual concerns subtly different
from those of his other Jesuit confrères on this topic,
and to what extent was this the result of the distinctiveness of Gregory of Nyssa's own rendition of the
theme? Is there even the suspicion of a certain rivalry
or tension between Daniélou, Rahner, and Balthasar
in responding (or failing explicitly to respond) to the
special importance of Gregory of Nyssa in this whole
story of 'spiritual sensation'? I think so, although the
evidences remain subtle and elusive.[36]

---

35  We now have available in published form the long cor-
    respondence of de Lubac and Daniélou: *Correspondance:
    1939–1974* (Paris, Cerf, 2021), which throws much light on
    their mutual interests in exegesis and reforming theology.

36  There is a certain mystery about why von Balthasar never
    chose to write anything specific about 'spiritual sense' in
    Nyssen, despite the fact that we know that he already read
    (and later translated) texts from the last, exegetical, com-
    mentaries of Nyssen alongside de Lubac and Daniélou at
    Fourvière, and also that his own, normative, view of 'spiri-
    tual sense' came to have a form very similar to Nyssen's own
    (at least as I read him: see *intra*, and n. 50, below). Mark J

Here we move, then, to the second section of our lecture (which, as we shall see, will in turn be crucial for the bridge to our final and third section on contemporary epistemology), and to a brief re-examination of Nyssen's quite unique teaching on the topic of 'spiritual sense'.

For the sake of necessary concision, I shall here make only *three* core interpretative points about

---

McInroy addresses this mystery briefly in *Balthasar and the Spiritual Senses*, 49–53, but without any definitive solution to the problem. My own proposal is that von Balthasar, who published his own monograph on Nyssen in 1942 (after a preliminary and lengthy article on him in 1939: see n. 22, above), was well aware that his friend Daniélou was at the same time completing his doctorate on the same patristic author, but himself forbore to expatiate on the 'spiritual senses' theme, instead focusing on the 'philosophical' dimensions of Nyssen's thought rather than his so-called 'mysticism'. In turn, Daniélou barely mentions Balthasar's monograph in his own doctoral thesis on Nyssen (which appeared the next year, in 1944), citing it in the bibliography but quoting it just once in relation to the question of Nyssen's 'abandonment' of Platonism in his embrace of the Philonic theme of divine 'darkness' (see *Platonisme et Théologie Mystique*, 170–171). We have a sense, then, of two Jesuit colleagues slightly defensively dancing around the same topic, but shying away from stepping on each other's toes. It is also significant that Rahner, in his first article on 'spiritual sense' (already discussed above), likewise failed to see the importance and distinctiveness of Nyssen's rendition of this topic: for more on that parallel 'mystery' of omission, see n. 39, below.

Gregory of Nyssa's *'doctrine* of spiritual sense,'[37] since the first thing one has to acknowledge is that it is far less systematized or clarified than this term ('the doctrine') would suggest, or indeed one might like it to be. But that does not mean that we cannot provide a careful and nuanced exegetical account of how Gregory's views appear to have developed and changed on this theme throughout his writing career as a philosopher and theologian.

First, there is the continuing debate about how Origen's and Gregory of Nyssa's account of 'spiritual sensation' relate or compare, since it is evident in some texts that Gregory is drawing on Origen directly (especially in his Prologue to the *Commentary on the Song of Songs*), and may even at times have Origen's text open in front of him as he is writing.[38] It is probably for that reason that Rahner

---

37  So described by Daniélou throughout *Platonisme et Théologie Mystique* , utilizing Rahner's term as earlier applied to Origen.

38  This is particularly obvious in both author's respective 'Prologues' to their commentaries on the *Song of Songs*; indeed Gregory explicitly cites Origen in his own: see *Gregory of Nyssa: Homilies on the Song of Songs*, translated with an Introduction and Notes by Richard A. Norris, Jr. (Atlanta, GA, Society of Biblical Literature, 2012), 11–13 (*In Cant.*, Prol., *GNO* vol. VI, 12–13), for his first direct citation of Origen; but even from the start of the Prologue it is obvious that he is aware of Origen's opening rendition of the text. With this compare *Origen: The Song of Songs*

makes some throw-away remarks at the end of his first (1932) essay on 'spiritual sensation' to the effect that Gregory of Nyssa's position is effectively the same as Origen's;[39] but on closer inspection this judgement is certainly misleading. The baton soon

------

Commentary and Homilies, translated and annotated by R. P. Lawson (New York, Newman Press, 1956), 'Prologue', 21–57, esp. 23–9 (PG 13. 65A-67A).

    To complement Norris's relatively recent edition and translation into English of Gregory's *Song* commentary, the new *Sources Chrétiennes* edition, translated into French and edited with notes by Mariette Canévet (with Françoise Vinel), is also to be commended, but so far only goes to the end of Homily V: Grégoire de Nysse, *Homélies sur le Cantique des Cantiques*, Tome I (Paris, Éditions du Cerf, 2021) —see 68–72 for introductory comments on the relation of Origen and Nyssen on 'spiritual sense'.

39  Rahner simply writes that the 'influence of Origen upon Gregory of Nyssa' is 'obvious', and adds: 'In his exposition of the Song of Songs the theory of the five spiritual faculties is explicitly represented as a teaching of the "philosophy" of the Song of Songs.' He then adds rather abruptly and oddly in closing (though only in the German version of the article), 'Further evidence is here unnecessary' (*Theological Investigations*, vol. XVI, 102). It has to be wondered (see n. 36, above) whether this cursory treatment of Nyssen by Rahner distracted von Balthasar too from a more intensive investigation of Nyssen's distinctive teaching on the topic of 'spiritual sense', although the fact that Balthasar read the later commentary work of Gregory with both de Lubac and Daniélou at Fourvière would count against such a hypothesis.

fell to Daniélou to investigate further, and to correct
this over-hasty assessment. However, his own exegesis of the theme of 'spiritual sense' in his celebrated
early monograph on Gregory, *Platonism et Théologie Mystique,* is to a large extent restricted to the
unfolding of the topic in Gregory's last exegetical
and 'spiritual' works—*The Life of Moses,* and more
especially the *Commentary on the Song.*[40] The result
is that a particular two-pronged emphasis here is
placed by Daniélou in his rendition of Nyssen's
application of this tradition *in distinction from Origen.* First, he points to Gregory's stress on visual or
noetic *darkness* as the seeming apex of the 'spiritual'
or 'mystical' ascent, as in Moses's entry into the 'dark
cloud' as he climbs Mt. Sinai (and here the influence
is definitely more from Philo rather than Origen);
and then, secondly, he points out a compensatory
excitation, intensification and purification of the
so-called 'lower senses' (touch, smell, taste) in terms
of the 'erotic' narratives of the *Song* commentary.
The overall impression given, then, is that the 'spiritual sense doctrine' is designed by Gregory of Nyssa
precisely to describe the *highest* states in 'mysticism'

---

40  Earlier texts in Gregory's *oeuvre* are of course occasionally
    cited, *en passant,* in Daniélou's monograph, but it is the
    last commentary texts which are focused upon especially
    in his treatment of 'spiritual sense', being the neglected ones
    which the de Lubac reading group had concentrated on at
    Fourvière.

and 'the spiritual life' (Daniélou's own oft-repeated terms); and indeed that the final ascent in Nyssen's spiritual scheme of the transformation of sense is not to enlightenment and noetic union (as in Origen) but to increasing and indeed impenetrable—but notably 'eroticized'—noetic darkness, in which the only option for human response is now a *reversal* of the usual prioritizing of sight as the indicator of intellectual achievement, and a new honing of the so-called lower senses as a means both of compensation and of bodily integration.[41]

Although Daniélou ramified and very slightly revised this account in later writing,[42] the fundamental picture presented of the import of 'spiritual sensation' in *Platonisme et Théologie Mystique* does not change radically.[43] Origen and Nyssen

---

41  See 'Les sens spirituels', in *Platonisme et Théologie Mystique*, 235–266. (It is notable that Rahner's first article, as well as Poulain's seminal work, are repeatedly cited in this section of Daniélou's monograph.)

42  Notably in the English publication, ed. Herbert Musurillo, *From Glory to Glory* (New York, Scribner's, 1961), with an important introduction by Daniélou and a wide selection of short translated texts from Nyssen, including a short section on 'the spiritual senses' (156–157).

43  I am grateful to William Daniel, *Christ the Liturgy* (Brooklyn, NY, Angelico Press, 2020), for his critique of my earlier 'Gregory of Nyssa' article on the 'spiritual senses', and his goad thereby to expand and refine it. In fact I do not find in *From Glory to Glory* any major developments or changes

are after different 'spiritual' goals with their teaching on spiritual sense, from this perspective,[44] with
Daniélou clearly approving, and advocating for,
Nyssen as an anticipator (as he sees it) of much of
the teaching of the later John of the Cross. But we
note that this 'mystical' analysis tends to distract
from any underlying *philosophical* import that
Nyssen's theory of 'spiritual sensation' might also
have had all along.

So persuasive and attractive is Daniélou's account
of the teaching of Nyssen in relation to Origen,
however, that it took me several years to become
aware that (at least on this topic of 'spiritual sense')
it was not *quite right*, and that for more than one reason. Let me explain.

First, a close reading of Nyssen's *Commentary on
the Song* reveals that the theme of noetic darkness
in *The Life of Moses* is not consistently maintained
in that slightly-later text, and indeed—as Martin

---

to Daniélou's rendition of 'spiritual sense' in Nyssen, but he
does clarify there (*contra* Rahner, though without chiding
him) that Gregory had 'inherited [the doctrine of spiritual sense] from Origen, and *developed [it] quite extensively*'
(*From Glory to Glory*, 25, my emphasis).

44 Daniélou does not make a great deal of this comparison;
but he does see Nyssen as anticipating John of the Cross
on the darkness of the 'nights' (*Platonisme et Théologie Mystique*, 209, 304; *From Glory to Glory*, 32), rather than link-
ing him to the Ignatian tradition, as Rahner wished to do
out of the Origenistic sources on 'spiritual sensation'.

Laird OSA has well pointed out in his own monograph on Gregory of Nyssa[45]—the light of noetic
*illumination* is actually more prominently promised
at key points in the *Song* commentary.[46] For Nyssen
himself, that is, Moses's 'dark cloud' is the precursor
to a more paradoxical combination of illumination
and darkness in the *Song* commentary (such as is
also characteristic of the works of the ps.-Diony-
sius, a little later on, with his characteristic talk of

---

45   Martin Laird, *Gregory of Nyssa and the Grasp of Faith:
Union, Knowledge and Divine Presence* (Oxford, O.U.P.,
2004), see esp. ch. 7, 174–204. Laird's treatment of Gregory's *Song* commentary has the merit of not being overde-
termined by Daniélou's earlier treatment, and by drawing
attention thereby to the features in it which go *beyond* the
account of darkness in *The Life of Moses*. See also the discerning discussion in Alessandro Cortesi, OP, *Le Omelie sul
Cantico dei Cantici di Gregorio di Nyssa* (Rome, Institutum
Patristicum Augustinianum, 2000) esp. ch. 5, 171–203.

46   See especially *In Cant.* VI (Norris, *Homilies*, Homily 6,
182–211 [GNO vol. VI, 171–199]), in relation to which
Daniélou only discusses the parallel darkness motif, also
present in this same Homily. Here (see esp. Norris, *Homilies*, 193–7 [GNO vol. VI, 180–183]) Nyssen presents a
particularly interesting combination of the two themes,
appealing both to a 'clear grasp of what is revealed', and
an equal insistence that 'I am seeking what is hidden in
darkness'. These two motifs are paradoxically related, to
be sure, but never illogically so for Nyssen, since—as he
explains in this crucial passage—*union* with the divine, as
an erotic consummation, goes beyond the mind's grasp, and
is achieved by the 'grasp of faith'.

'luminous darkness'). Secondly, however, and more significantly, the particular concentration on Nyssen's last exegetical works by Daniélou, whilst not misleading in its exegesis of special states of what Gregory calls 'mingling' with Christ (which constitute for him the *apex* of the life of purified and transformed sensation), fails to take full account of the exposition of the 'spiritual sense' theme building over many years in his earlier writings.

For in fact, Gregory's teaching on this theme of 'spiritual sense' stirs early (with strong evocations of those elements in Origen's writing in which physical and spiritual senses are seen as initially radically disjunct in the Christian battle against sin);[47] then it

---

47  For this disjunctive rendition of 'spiritual sense' in Origen, see, e.g., *De principiis*, I.I.9 (*PG* 11. 129B-130A), trans. G. W. Butterworth (London, S.P.C.K., 1936), 14; and *Contra Celsum* VII.43 (*PG* 11. 1484A), trans. Henry Chadwick (Cambridge, C.U.P., 1965), 431. For similarly disjunctive expressions of the relation of physical and spiritual sense in Nyssen, see my discussion of the relevant texts from the earlier writings of Nyssen on spiritual sense in 'Gregory of Nyssa', 53, n. 56, including 'On Virginity', XI. 20–25 (*GNO* vol. VIII/I, 292), and 'Treatise on the Inscriptions of the Psalms', 6.45, 8.76 (*GNO* vol. V, 41, 52). It should be acknowledged that this dualistic rendition of 'sense' and 'spirit' does not *disappear* in the later writings of Nyssen, precisely because it the great mark of the ongoing battle between (negative) passion and purified desire, which is a life-long undertaking (see, e.g., Norris, *Homilies*, 329–331, at the close of Homily 10 [*GNO* vol. VI, 313–4]). However,

comes to the fore in his 'middle period' (from about the time of his brother Basil's death in 379 CE), in a more subtle and distinctive *philosophical* form (which I shall focus on shortly); and then it develops and changes yet more throughout the last fifteen years or so of his life, as his *theological* enunciation of it comes to its climax in his last exegetical works (on which Daniélou expatiates). But what he says about it in his last works, whilst in some cases correcting and modifying Origen, as Daniélou already

---

as I argue afresh in what follows here, it would I believe be quite misleading to follow Mark Edwards in his recent assertion that Gregory's 'exegesis is *governed throughout* by a polar opposition of flesh and intellect' (Mark Edwards, 'Origen and Gregory of Nyssa on the Song of Songs', in eds. Anna Marmodoro and Neil B. McLynn, *Exploring Gregory of Nyssa: Philosophical, Theological, and Historical Studies* (Oxford, O.U.P., 2018), at 87, my emphasis). That is to ignore many intricate aspects of his epistemology and soteriology which I here expound afresh. Likewise, Hans Boersma's short discussion of Gregory on 'spiritual sense' in his *Embodiment and Virtue in Gregory of Nyssa: An Anagogical Approach* (Oxford, O.U.P., 2013), 93–100, misses, in my view, much of the subtlety and distinctiveness of Gregory's account of the body-soul relation in this doctrine, such that he can start by asserting that, 'The recent focus on the body would have struck Gregory as odd' (93). However, he does acknowledge in closing that 'The bodily senses are important to Gregory precisely because they allow for a *transposition* to spiritual perception' (99–100, my emphasis)—a point that he does not spell out in detail.

implied,[48] also has other notable and continuing features still in *common* with Origen.[49] This is because Origen himself is certainly misread if we see his full account of 'spiritual sense' as straightforwardly *negative* towards the 'body', given that —following Paul in 1 Corinthians 15— even this mortal body must ultimately be *en route*, in some mysterious sense, to

---

48  I would see this both in Gregory's claiming that this teaching *is* genuinely open, *contra* Origen, to the 'fleshly-minded' who genuinely seek to purify and integrate their senses (Norris, *Homilies*, 2–3 [GNO vol. VI, 3–4]), and—as Daniélou also noted—in his glorifying in a new way the potential even of the transformed lower senses for union with Christ in an intimate 'darkness' (see, e.g., Norris, *Homilies*, Homily 1, 37 [GNO vol. VI, 34–36], and Homily 6, 193 [GNO vol. VI, 180–81]).

49  This is not so surprising, because both authors, depending on the context of their writing, can at one moment speak *disjunctively* of 'sense' and 'spirit' when indicating the ongoing battle between sin and salvation, but simultaneously stress the transformative *passage* of the embodied person from one state to the other. As Mark J. McInroy shows in 'Origin of Alexandria', 28–33, even in Origen's 'early' writings (in particular, in the *De principiis*) we may find an apparent contradiction between talk of a straightforward disjunction between 'mortal' and 'immortal' senses (I, 1.9 [PG 11. 129C], Butterworth, 14), on the one hand, and then talk of an 'advance' from one to the other (IV, 4. 10 [PG 11.412C-414A], Butterworth, 327–8), on the other. It is undeniable that the former trope is more common in Origen, but the latter is by no means absent.

its 'spiritual' transformation in the resurrection.[50] In sum, the relationship between Origen's teaching on 'spiritual sense' and Gregory's is much more complicated and contrapuntal than I, at any rate, once thought, and even averred in my own earlier writing, when I was most strongly under the influence of Daniélou himself.

Now I see it somewhat differently. It is not that Origen's view of 'spiritual sense' is 'metaphorical' in relation to the physical body and Gregory's 'analogical' (these categories indeed represent an anachronistic Thomist disjunction originally pressed by Poulain and brought clunkily from there into Rahner's influential early discussion[51]). Nor is it

---

50  As a penetrating recent comparison by Elisa Zocchi of Rahner's and Balthasar's rendition of Origen's understanding of 'spiritual sense' reveals, the two modern authors diverged in interpretation most importantly on the issue of how to construe *direct* 'spiritual sensation' of the divine, and whether it must involve a truly 'incarnational' understanding of the resurrection body itself, on which matter Balthasar insisted on *some* sort of continuum between the physical body and the spiritual, citing *De principiis*, III, 6.6 (Butterworth, 251–2). Balthasar did however acknowledge Origen's inconsistency on this point: see Elisa Zocchi, *The Sacramentality of the World and the Mystery of Freedom: Hans Urs von Balthasar, Reader of Origin* (Münster, Aschendorff Verlag, 2021), 177–208.

51  See again Mark. J. McInroy's analysis of this long-standing interpretative problem in his 'Origen of Alexandria', which

that Nyssen's teaching integrates the 'body' to the spirit while Origen's does not, as I myself wrongly held earlier[52] (since both thinkers are complex, rich and elusive on this point, as any rendition of 1 Corinthians 15 on the 'resurrection body' perforce must be). Rather, Nyssen's teaching on 'spiritual sense', whilst inheriting much from Origen's, has, I believe, both a *philosophical* and a *theological* dimension which is distinctive to him. It involves, first, a general philosophical/epistemic theory of how sensuality (even 'fleshly' sensuality as corruptible by sin) is *worked with* at base in order for a progressive growth in the soul to occur; and then, secondly, a correlative theological vision of the higher stages of this disconcerting sensual re-orientation, in which the normal 'hierarchy' of the senses is indeed upended, and the soul/body already prepared for its future resurrection state, such that we may indeed even glimpse it anticipatorily in the dying phases of a holy life.

What is crucial for understanding Gregory's distinctive version of the teaching on 'spiritual sensation', then, is that what he lays out in the last

---

he attempts to dissolve by declaring the disjunction between 'metaphorical' and 'analogical' inadequate to deal with the subtlety and malleability of Origen's forms of expression.

52 As, for instance, in my *Powers and Submissions: Philosophy, Spirituality and Gender* (Oxford, Blackwell, 2002), 137–138.

commentary works about the actual unitive 'mingling' with Christ comes only after long preparatory development on the lower slopes of moral, intellectual *and* sensual purification.[53] In short, the development of the life of virtue *is* the development of the life of both intellectual *and* sensory transformation for Gregory: it is a whole theory, both 'philosophical' and 'theological', of how body and soul are together *en route* to God, together already beginning to enact now what the *resurrection* body will one day be like in its full glory. And where Gregory sounds a particularly daring note here is that for him even our corruptible 'flesh' (*sarx*) itself—represented by the 'garments of skin' which were the cost of the

---

53 This is why Nyssen's language of 'spiritual sensation' can be found in discussions of all three of the 'stages of ascent' (*ethikē*, *physikē*, and *enoptikē*) which Gregory inherited from Origen. The first is characterized by the ongoing battle of 'flesh' and 'spirit' for moral virtue; the second by rising to a perception of divine order and beauty in the world as a whole; the third by actual 'union' with Christ. For a highly-suggestive and insightful account of these three 'stages' as understood by Nyssen, see Andrew Louth, *The Origins of the Christian Mystical Tradition: From Plato to Denys* (Oxford, Clarendon Press, 1981), 80–97. However, Louth's account is (acknowledgedly) highly indebted to Daniélou's reading of Nyssen, and thus implicitly critiqued by what I expound in this account: we should not be restricted in our interpretation of these three 'stages' in what Gregory implies of them in his *Life of Moses*. See, in particular, Norris, *Homilies*, Homily 1, 18–19 (GNO VI, 17).

Fall[54]—becomes the paradoxical *means* of such
transformation; the physical body is thus not merely
a 'dress rehearsal' format which must ultimately be
*replaced* by the resurrection 'body' (the 'spiritual'
*sōma* of 1 Corinthians 15. 44), but can in the lives
of holy people even be glimpsed as already present
in their dying physicality. It was this that Gregory
claimed to see in his sister Macrina in her passage to
death (in his wonderful narrative, *The Life of Macrina*);[55] and this in itself has implications, I suggest,

---

54  Gregory spells out his unique understanding of the salvific
    'use' to be made of the 'garments of skin' in his *Catechetical
    Oration*, trans. in ed. Edward Rochie Hardy, *Christology of
    the Later Fathers* (London, S.C.M., 1964), 282–286 (GNO
    III/IV, 29–36), insisting that the 'sentient' part of the
    human is not to be 'destroyed' but 'used' or 'remolded' in the
    'restoration of man'. Daniélou himself draws attention to
    the radicality of this rendition of the Fall, but does not link
    it specifically to the 'spiritual sense' theme: see *From Glory
    to Glory*, 12–13.

55  I have discussed Gregory's views on Macrina and the res-
    urrection body more closely in *Powers and Submissions*,
    161–166, drawing on a rich earlier discussion in Caroline
    Walker Bynum, *The Resurrection of the Body in Western
    Christianity, 200-1336* (New York, Columbia U.P., 1995),
    81–86. For Gregory's description of Macrina's last hours
    and how she appeared 'to belong no longer in the world of
    men', see 'The Life of Macrina', trans. Virginia Woods Cal-
    lahan, in *Saint Gregory of Nyssa: Ascetical Works* (Wash-
    ington, DC, Catholic University of America Press, 1967),
    179–181, at 179 (see GNO VIII/I, 395–398).

for the distinctiveness and originality of his understanding of 'spiritual sensation' more generally.

So much for the complex and subtle points of
different emphasis between Nyssen and Origen
on 'spiritual sense'. But this brings me immediately
to my second, and correlated, exegetical point in
this section. And that is that we need more consistently to search Gregory's whole *oeuvre* for the
distinctive *language* of 'spiritual sensation' ('the
sense of the soul', the 'eye of the soul', the 'hearing
of the heart', and other cognate phrases such as the
Pauline 'inner man') in order to glean a complete
picture of how his own thinking developed on this
theme over time, especially in relation to his own
deepening spiritual maturity and insight. In my
earlier treatment of this challenge,[56] I made the
first attempt at such a sweep, based on an exhaus-
tive *Thesaurus Linguae Graecae* search for these
key words and phrases across all Nyssen's works.
It was on this basis that I was able to assert that
Gregory's remarkable 'middle-phase' work, *On the
Soul and the Resurrection*,[57] written around the
time of his sister Macrina's death, marks a crucial
moment of transition in Gregory's own particular
thinking about the *integration* of bodily sense with

---

56  See again, 'Gregory of Nyssa', in *The Spiritual Senses*, 36–55.

57  See 'Gregory of Nyssa', 42–29. I have condensed here my
   recapitulation of that more extended discussion.

the soul, *en route* to later resurrection life. It seems
it is the recent death of his brother, Basil, and the
imminent threat of the death of his beloved sister, Macrina, that first educes this new and highly
original teaching in Nyssen's distinctive form. The
text is confected as an actual dialogue of Gregory
with Macrina, in which, after together considering
and rejecting a whole range of pagan philosophical accounts of the nature of the soul, Gregory
returns at last to the elusive 'spiritual' resurrection
body of 1 Corinthians 15 as the rightful hope for
all Christians, and also that which even now we
start to yearn towards and *live*. We shall all 'pass
through the Fire', as he puts it, but be born again
in our 'original splendour', in the full 'perfection of
bodiliness.'[58] It is largely through the dying Macrina's mouth, however (*hē didaskolos*, 'the 'teacher',
as Gregory calls her here) that the explicit view
is expressed, even already at the start of the dialogue, that it is by working *with* our senses (not
against them) that we move towards perfection in
virtue. As Macrina puts it: it is 'by the very oper-
ation of our senses we are led to conceive of that

---

58  See 'On the Soul and the Resurrection', trans. W. Moore
    and H. A Wilson, *NPNF*, series 2, vol. V (Grand Rapids,
    MI, Eerdmans, 1979), 467–8 (*GNO* XV, 121, 123): this
    whole final passage of the dialogue makes very clear Gregory's
    *organic* and *purificatory* perception of how the resurrection
    body emerges from the physical body.

reality and intelligence that surpasses our senses.'[59] In other words, the life of sanctification *is* the life of sensual and indeed 'erotic' transformation (in Gregory's particular understanding of the unending *erōs*—desire—that propels the Christian life); and this is a life not of the final suppression or rejection of passions, either, but of their intensification, unification and purification (as Gregory had anticipatorily averred as early as his first extraordinary work 'On Virginity'[60]). It is a life, as he explains elsewhere in his reflections on Matthew 25, that should ultimately issue in its maturity in a seeking for Christ

---

59  Here I prefer the translation of Catherine Roth, *On the Soul and the Resurrection* (Crestwood, NY, St. Vladimir's Seminary Press), 34 (*GNO* XV, 13). Von Balthasar comments explicitly on this passage in his *Presence and Thought*, 49, and so remarks therefrom: 'Is Gregory therefore an idealist or a Platonist? An idealist, yes. A Platonist, no, or, at least, only in certain limited respects. His philosophy is situated boldly between Plato and Aristotle'. (It should be noted that this assessment is very far from that of Mark Edwards, see n. 47, *supra*.)

60  See especially Gregory's use of the Platonic 'hydraulic' metaphor in 'On Virginity', VII (Moore and Wilson, *NPNF*, series 2, vol V, 352 [*GNO* VIII/I, 280–281]), to indicate the importance of 'erotic', passionate, power being purified and unified rather than dispersed. For a discussion of this theme in the early Nyssen in relation to contemporary ascetical concerns, see my *The New Asceticism: Sexuality, Gender and the Quest for God* (London, Bloomsbury, 2015), 29–53.

not only in the pages of Scripture, in contemplation, or in the sacraments, but in the fleshly faces of the poor and the sick, by so attuning one's *sensorium* to the presence of Christ there that one is 'mingled' with him in precisely the acts of mercy to which his presence calls us.[61]

If what I have so far sketched about Gregory's teaching on 'spiritual sense' is correct, then it leads me to my third and last reflection on his significance and originality, from which we shall be able to segue quickly into our promised consideration of the potential application of his theory to contemporary concerns. And this last point is something that has become clear to me only in my own more recent reconsideration of Gregory's *Commentary on the Song of Songs*, having freed myself from my earlier over-gullibility towards Daniélou's brilliant, but partial, rendition of this text. For now[62] I see

---

61  For the relevant texts in Nyssen on Matthew 25 and philanthropy to the poor, see Adrianus van Heck, *Gregorii Nysseni de Pauperibus Orationes Duo* (Leiden, Brill, 1964), and the excellent article by Brian E. Daley, SJ, 'Building a New City: The Cappadocian Fathers and the Rhetoric of Philanthropy', *Journal of Early Christian Studies* 7 (1999), 431–61.

62  See Sarah Coakley, 'Gregory of Nyssa on Spiritual Ascent and Trinitarian Orthodoxy: A Reconsideration of the Relation between Doctrine and *Askesis*', in eds. Giulio Maspero and Miguel Brugarolas, *Gregory of Nyssa's In Canticum*, XII International Colloquium on Gregory of Nyssa (Leiden, Brill, 2018), 360–375.

properly for the first time that, for Gregory, growth
in virtue, sensual purification, and transformed
understanding of doctrinal truths, are all correla-
tively developmental *at the same time* according to
his mature and final understanding of the Christian life. Hence doctrinal truth, for Gregory, even
truth about the Trinity, is also not enunciated on a
'flat plane' (as I termed it earlier); it is not received,
that is, merely propositionally or credally, but *in
via* towards 'union' and divine 'ecstasy', as he now
puts it.[63] The way the Christian even understands
the fundamental truth of God-as-Trinity, therefore, will *change* along this transformative path,
precisely according to the developments of 'spiritual sense'. This in turn means that the Spirit's
invitation of us into participation in the life of
God signals a *progressive* 'mingling' with Christ;
and this is a development which might suggest a
loss of fully externalized, expository, trinitarian
thinking, but which Gregory would now see quite
differently. For this is precisely the point at which
extrinsic *theorization* about the Trinity issues now
in *incorporation* by the Spirit into the life of God
(in Christ) itself. Gregory appeals repeatedly here
to the logic of Paul's account of ecstatic prayer in
Romans 8, in which we are here 'adopted' into the

---

63 See especially *In Cant.* IV (Norris, *Homilies*, Homily 4,
   120–121[GNO VI, 108]); and also compare Homily 6,
   192–193 (GNO VI, 180–181).

divine life through the Spirit's intervention.[64] Thus, what we now in the modern period artificially distinguish intellectually as 'Trinitarianism' and 'Christology' are inseparable for Gregory, just as the life of virtue and spiritual accord becomes inseparable from the project of a purified and unified *sensorium*, attuned to that same Christ.

Needless to say, as Gregory fully acknowledges, and gently underscores in the third homily of his *Song* commentary, it follows that not everyone in this progression is in the same position along this journey into God: 'For the child who was born for us—Jesus, who within those who receive him grows in a variety of different ways in wisdom and stature and grace—is not the same in all but indwells in a way that accords with the capacity of the one in whom he comes . . .'[65] This is a challenging and perhaps discomforting thought, but it is an inexorable accompaniment to Nyssen's mature thinking about 'spiritual sensation': that the extent of our capacity to manifest Christ to others resides in our own level of graced sensitivity and receptivity to Christ *in others*, honed by the Spirit. And underlyingly, to put it now in other and more 'secular' terms, it is a question thus of how much *reality* we can truly bear, can truly attend to through our senses, intellectual cognition, and moral responsiveness.

---

64  Norris, *Homilies*, Homily 4, 128–129 (GNO VI, 115–116).

65  Norris, *Homilies*, Homily 3, 106–107 (GNO VI, 96–97).

But if it is sensitive, courageous, attention to the physical, personal and moral realities of the world that is the fundamental *philosophical* issue at stake here, then the importance of Nyssen's insights into the wider realms of epistemology— potentially beyond even the Christian fold and into the so-called modern 'secular'—is what must now engage us. And this is not far-fetched, even from Gregory's own perspective, as I have here argued; after all, it was he and Macrina who together agreed on the philosophical demand and costliness of becoming, over a life-time, 'large-souled', as opposed to 'small-souled'—that is, working with the 'senses' to move 'beyond the senses' into all truth.[66]

And that brings us at last to our third and last section of this lecture, and to a seemingly very different context and range of contemporary challenges for the Church and our culture.

### III. NYSSEN'S THEORY AND ITS POTENTIAL CONTEMPORARY IMPORT: ON RACISM, SEXISM AND THE PORNOGRAPHIC PROBLEM OF SEEING/'SENSING' THE 'OTHER'

So what, if anything, could now be rescued and utilized for today from this extraordinary vision of

---

66  Roth, *On the Soul and Resurrection*, 31–32 (GNO XV, 9), 34–35 (GNO XV, 13–14).

'spiritual sensation' in Gregory of Nyssa's works? How might we apply it to our contemporary sensual lives, formed as they are not only by the evidences of goodness, beauty and truth that our education and spiritual formation, at their best, aim to attune us to, but which are also constantly manipulated by visual propaganda, advertisements, online gaming, *Netflix*, social media, and readily-available pornography? And how, in particular, can we relate this ancient tradition of 'spiritual sensation' to the *distorted* perceptual worlds of culturally-ingrained racism, sexism, and the notable pornographic propulsion to eroticize visual images of objectified and devalued bodies?

Let me start this last section of my lecture by trying to defend my earlier proposal that these three problems (racism, sexism and pornography) belong together, a thought that may not be welcome, let alone familiar. Yet we shall be assisted here by some fascinating new philosophical developments in contemporary analytic epistemology. From there, and in closing, I shall offer some speculative and programmatic suggestions for beginning to re-think these contemporary problems in the light of the 'spiritual sense' tradition, and Gregory of Nyssa's rendition of it in particular.

It is only recently, first, that what some now call the '*problem of seeing*' has come to the fore in philosophical reflections on the nature of racism as an embedded cultural phenomenon.[67] We tend to think of racism, and rightly, as a social, political and economic issue—one, fundamentally, therefore of 'rights', of access to education and other forms of privilege and financial advantage from which non-'whites' may still continue to be barred, covertly or overtly. But what if racism is also (and precisely as a result of hard-to-pinpoint social and personal conditioning), a more profoundly *epistemic* and *perceptual* problem, all the way down? The anguishing spectacle of so many 'black' bodies shot, or beaten, or suffocated, in cold blood in the United States in recent years does not simply raise the issue of how police are institutionally trained to deal, generically, with persons they regard as suspicious or as potentially violent; for it also presses the deeper question of how they differentiatedly

---

67  In a recent philosophical essay on 'spiritual perception', I have analyzed this issue more closely in relation to recent police shootings of young 'black' men in the USA: see 'Spiritual Perception and the Racist Gaze: Can Contemplation Shift Racism?', in eds. Frederick Aquino and Paul L. Gavrilyuk, *Perceiving Things Divine: Towards a Constructive Account of Spiritual Perception* (Oxford, OUP, 2022), 153–176. This study may be read as a cognate essay to the current undertaking, in that the classic spiritual materials I focus on there are the writings of the 16th century Carmelites, whose thematic interests Daniélou rightly sees as anticipated in some key elements of Gregory of Nyssa's writing.

*see* such persons (as 'white' or 'black' or 'brown'[68]) in the first place. And when we reach too quickly— as is now standard—for the catch-all category of 'implicit bias'[69] to explain such troubling phenomena, we run the risk of obfuscating the problem yet further—of associating it with a sort of mysterious 'spookiness' in which individual moral agency is once again curiously obscured by an appeal to unassailable yet completely unconscious forces.

---

68  I am somewhat resistant to the 'essentializing' features of this 'colour'-language, even though it has now become normalized, indeed even 'politically correct', in contemporary North America. My use of 'scare-quotes', then, indicates a semantic and philosophical discussion that remains to be had on this front. Not only is it often hard to say who 'qualifies' for these categorizations, but many other categories would seem to be needed to cater for all. So we need to probe what 'identarian' purpose they are serving. For more on the contemporary political and philosophical problems of 'identarianism', see my forthcoming *Sin, Racism and Divine Darkness: An Essay 'On Human Nature'* (Cambridge, C.U.P.).

69  Michael Brownstein, 'Implicit Bias', https://plato.stanford. edu/entries/implicit-bias/ (accessed March 30, 2022) maps out the multiple philosophical *conundra*, epistemological and moral, that are raised by appeal to this supposed phenomenon. That does not mean, of course, that (unconscious) 'implicit bias' does not exist—on the contrary; but it does caution against easy and superficial judgements based on psychological testing which are hard to verify empirically.

It is true that psychological tests have been developed (most famously at Harvard) to demonstrate the existence of such 'bias' in individuals, on the basis of just one quick computer test.[70] And other—more subtle—psychological research projects have sought to show how visual images

---

70  Recent studies of 'implicit bias' investigations, especially those emanating from the Harvard Psychology Department (the 'Implicit Association Test'), indicate that their empirical results are very hard to correlate with actual 'racist' behaviours: for an important survey article on these theoretical problems, citing relevant recent scholarly publications, see Jesse Singal, 'Psychology's Favorite Tool for Measuring Racism Isn't Up to the Job', https://www.thecut.com/2017/01/psychologys-racism-measuring-tool-isnt-up-to-the-job.html. We must underscore here also the paradoxical nature of the relation of the modern 'rights' tradition (centrally concerned with autonomy, freedom, conscious intentionality, 'Enlightenment'), to the equally-modern birth of psychoanalysis, and its attempted probing of the realm of the *unconscious*. Note that the problems of contemporary American racism sit notably astride these divergent, if not contradictory, directions in modern thought, leading to very different theoretic understandings of 'race'/racism and its problems. Of late, the liberal 'rights' tradition has come into outright conflict with 'identity politics' on precisely these issues: for a perceptive journalistic reflection on this *dénouement*, see *The Economist*, July 11, 2020, https://www.economist.com/international/2020/07/09/enlightenment-liberalism-is-losing-ground-in-the-debate-about-race.

of young black men, in particular, have become
culturally associated with violence or crime.[71] But
the trouble with such investigations, as their crit-
ics are not slow to point out, is that their meth-
odology is often either questionably inconsistent
or even circular;[72] and when a 'white'—or indeed
a 'black'—person has been triumphantly declared
'prejudiced' on the basis of an 'implicit bias' test,
what is to follow? If we arrive at the sort of conclusions proposed by Robin DiAngelo, in her celebrated book, *White Fragility*, that *all* 'white' people
are 'white supremacists', through and through,
and any attempt to deflect such a charge is mere
self-convicting 'denial' (so-called 'white fragility'),
we have succumbed to a viewpoint whereby all
the complexity of *differentiated* sensual accord to
moral reality (such as we glimpsed in Gregory of
Nyssa) is lost, and the deplored 'racial binary' of

---

71  This might involve, in philosophical terms, what is called
    'second-order' perceptual content, raising the problem of
    whether unconsciously-held prejudicial views may actually
    infect ocular vision itself (so-called 'cognitive penetration');
    for one recent examination of this supposed phenomenon
    within the context of racism, see Correll, J., Wittenbrink,
    B., Crawford, M. T., & Sadler, M. S. (2015), 'Stereotypic
    vision: How stereotypes disambiguate visual stimuli', *Jour-
    nal of Personality and Social Psychology*, 108(2015), 219–233
    (https://psycnet.apa.org/doi/10.1037/pspa0000015).

72  See again, n. 69.

our culture merely re-instantiated in an inverted but viciously re-ontologized form.[73]

No, the 'seeing' problem, surely, is more complex and deep than these one-off tests and psychological analyses allow; for if we cannot—for whatever reasons of inherited or socially-mandated prejudice—even *see* each other as individuals with 'rights', or—as Gregory of Nyssa put it more pointedly and theologically—as actually manifesting the 'face' of Christ before us, then it is clear that the 'seeing problem' is no mere prejudicial veneer that can be tweaked or shamed by an afternoon of mandatory consciousness-raising; nor is it satisfactorily exposed in all its complexity by a quick online 'implicit bias' test.

---

73 Robin DiAngelo, *White Fragility: Why It's So Hard for White People to Talk About Racism* (Boston, Beacon Press, 2018), has taken the 'liberal' consciousness by storm, and particularly, it seems, the liberal Christian consciousness. The book is profoundly committed to the view that 'white' and 'black' represent the only fixed 'binary' in American culture, and that all those who are 'white' are also 'white supremicists' (whilst of course also denying it). It is important to underscore DiAngelo's conclusions at the end of her book: 'a positive white identity is an impossible goal. White identity is inherently racist; white people do not exist outside the system of white supremacy' (*White Fragility*, 149). For a fractious critique of this book from a non-'white' perspective, see John McWhorter's 'The Dehumanizing Condescension of *White Fragility*', https://www.theatlantic.com/ideas/archive/2020/07/dehumanizing-condescension-white-fragility/614146/.

On the contrary, it is an issue for the visual sensorium that cuts all the way down, deep into our ever-changing spiritual and moral lives as much as also into our social and political and economic negotiations. The *problem*, then, is how to give a nuanced, differentiated, and philosophically-persuasive account of what is going on here.

Now, racism and *sexism* are of course by no means 'tokens of one type', as the philosophers would say: they cut across one another and intersect in disturbing ways, especially in the notable—and also often unconscious—eroticization of the specifically 'black' body, both male and female, in a culture of desire that is a kind of inverse manifestation of that same racism.[74] But from the perspective of a Gregory of Nyssa one might argue that sexism in its many contemporary forms also comes with a notable incapacity to 'see' and 'hear', and perhaps even to 'touch' and 'taste' and 'smell', as well: the evidence of bodies of different sexuality and gender and 'orientation' are arrayed before us, but what *is* it that prevents us from seeing all of these bodies as beloved of God, or as 'faces' (as the Jewish philosopher Emmanuel

---

74 See Amira Srinivasan, *The Right to Sex: Feminism in the Twenty-Frist Century* (New York, Farrar, Strauss and Giroux, 2021), for a disturbing and compelling *philosophical* analysis of how racism and sexism/sexual violence are integrally related and politically freighted at the same time in contemporary Western culture.

Lévinas would say) making equal ethical demands on us all?[75] The *Me Too* movement rightly focuses on actual acts of violence and abuse against women, both 'white' and 'black', and castigates the way that powerful men are able to mandate, normalize and conceal such acts. But the remaining problems of our sexualized and sexist culture are much wider and more profound than these more obvious aberrations; for—again—they go deep into the practices of 'seeing' and 'sensing' that are so familiar to us that they have even lost their capacity to shock.

It is here that I am struck afresh by the extraordinary way in which (even entirely legal, so-called 'soft') pornography tends to coarsen and intentionally 'objectify' the body of the 'other', creating an ever-increasing *habitus* of distance from moral identification with the sexual object, who in the predictable repetitions of pornographic visualization becomes a mere play-thing of fantasy and control. As my former philosophy colleague from Cambridge, Rae Langton, has repeatedly re-iterated in her tireless feminist work against 'objectifying' pornographic images, the so-called 'right' to submit one's fantasy life to this downward spiral of moral disconnection from empathy is a strange 'liberal' right

---

75 See Emmanuel Lévinas, *Totality and Infinity: An Essay on Exteriority* (orig., 1961; Kluwer Academic, Dordrecht, 1991).

indeed, founded on the extraordinary presumption that individualized, hedonistic pleasures are entirely 'private' and have no bearing whatever on ethical, social and political life more generally.[76] But once we understand the ethical significance of any 'habitus'— of what we repeatedly do so as to re-instantiate and reinforce a pattern of life (a 'training', therefore, of the senses in one direction or another) —how can we any longer deny that our extraordinary cultural addiction to pornography has importantly shared roots with our equally notable (and seemingly unshakeable) systems of racism and sexism?[77]

---

76 See Rae Langton, *Sexual Solipsism: Philosophical Essays on Pornography and Objectification* (Oxford, O.U.P., 2009). Of course, this view is controversial and debatable—and a significant sub-section of feminists think that there is (good?) pornography that can escape this charge. Langton puts up a strong argument, however, both against classic 'libertarians' like Ronald Dworkin, and post-modern gender theorists like Judith Butler, for the dangers of repetitious uses of pornography in inscribing messages of 'objectification' and 'hatred' against the bodies used to produce pornographic pleasure.

77 A recent Barna survey, 'Porn in the Digital Age' (https://www.barna.com/research/porn-in-the-digital-age-new-research-reveals-10-trends/) estimates that an increasing number of younger men, and a burgeoning group of younger women, are regular watchers of pornography, and that recent years have witnessed a radical shift to greater 'porn use'. Reliable statistics are hard to come by, but one Christian website (https://www.missionfrontiers.org/

I am moving fast here, of course, and very controversially too; but my aim throughout this lecture has simply been to unfurl preliminarily the thought of a deeper set of *sensual* problems that afflict our culture than we normally imagine, and to join some dots between issues which are often kept apart. To be sure, an enormous cluster of contentious philosophical issues are encoded here in what I have spoken of so briefly—but much progress in *analyzing* them out, at least, has been made of late. That is not the same as curing or healing them, of course, and that may be where the Church, more importantly, may fit in.

But this is therefore where I want to point here very briefly to a number of exciting recent developments in secular epistemology—almost all, interestingly, spearheaded by women philosophers—which

---

issue/article/15-mind-blowing-statistics-about-pornography-and-the-church) claims that '68% of church-going men and over 50% of pastors view porn on a regular basis', and '57% of pastors say porn addiction is the most damaging issue in their congregation. 69% say porn has adversely impacted the church'. It should be added that by now, according to the same survey, '87% of Christian women have watched porn'. An earlier church survey of pornography use (*Church Militant*, January 18, 2016) came up with even more startling statistics, especially for younger men and women: see https://www.churchmilitant.com/news/article/new-survey-of-porn-use-shows-startling-stats-for-men-and-women.

appear to be honing in from several different directions on these same set of moral and social issues, and their crucial sensual/perceptual manifestations; this work is, I believe, transforming analytic epistemology in the process.

In particular, and firstly, the philosophical analysis of the core issue of 'attention', which one might say goes back to Simone Weil's celebrated reflections on school-studies as a preparation for the profound pastoral attention that might be given to someone at the point of death,[78] has of late been ramified by feminist and other philosophical commentators in order to explore what *sort* of attention, exactly, is the best sort for perceptual and moral insight into those whose lot is literally 'overlooked' in our society. This has enormous implications, I need hardly say, for the issues of racism and sexism just outlined. Is the best and most morally-attuned 'attention', for instance, objective, dispassionate, contemplative, and 'Platonic', as Irish Murdoch memorably urged in *The Sovereignty of Good?*[79] Or is it passionately empathetic and selective, as others such as Rebecca Kukla have

---

78  Simone Weil, 'Reflections on the Right Use of School Studies with a View to the Love of God', in *Waiting on God* (London, Collins/Fontana, 1959), 66–76.

79  Iris Murdoch, *The Sovereignty of Good* (London, Routledge and Kegan Paul, 1970).

argued in riposte from a feminist perspective?[80] Either side of this ongoing debate is, clearly, concerned with moral outcomes and their perceptual accompaniments.

But further, when we ask ourselves, and inversely, how we can become (metaphorically) 'blind' to others' suffering, is it because we are distracted, selectively failing to concentrate, or somehow trained out of a more fulsome vison? Or is it, more worryingly still, that our perceptual faculties themselves are actually *invaded* by substantial prejudicial content—via the purported phenomenon of 'cognitive penetration' (an issue which continues to be hotly debated in philosophical discussions of perception)? It is here that the Harvard philosopher Susanna Siegel has made such significant—albeit controversial—inroads of late into the debates on perceptual racism by arguing that what we bring to our 'racialized' perceptions are *not*, after all, *beyond* rational analysis and adjudication (not vague and 'spooky' in the ways described above in relation to 'implicit bias'), but rather manifestations of underlying 'beliefs' which can indeed be excavated, discussed

---

80  Rebecca Kukla, 'Attention and Blindness: Objectivity and Contingency in Moral Perception', *Canadian Journal of Philosophy* 28 (2002), 319–346. I discuss Kukla's alternative feminist approach in 'Spiritual Perception and the Racist Gaze' (see n. 66, above).

and rationally evaluated.[81] In a similar way, but at a different level of epistemological analysis, Miranda Fricker's ground-breaking work on 'testimonial' and 'hermeneutic' injustice[82] has begun to frame a new philosophical analysis of how the dispossessed in our society can be reduced to feeling not only that their own accounts (about racism and sexism, for instance) are not received as worthy of attention by the philosophic and legal powers-that-be (this Fricker calls 'testimonial injustice'), but how they themselves have often been reduced to a position where they do not trust their *own* personal authority to name such wrongs (her so-called 'hermeneutical injustice'). Simply to name and describe such phenomena—to give them *epistemic* freightage—is already to puncture the silence with which such evidences have been treated in the past, even in formal court settings. When we add to this body of epistemological investigation the insights of those philosophers who, in Rae Langton's train, are probing the ills of pornographic 'speech' and its visualizing and moral impacts, especially in relation to sexism and racism (often here combined), we begin to see all the more clearly the entangled

---

81  Susanna Siegel, *The Rationality of Perception* (Oxford, O.U.P., 2017), esp. 177–196.

82  Miranda Fricker, *Epistemic Injustice: Power & the Ethics of Knowing* (Oxford, O.U.P., 2007).

web of racist, sexist and pornographic visualization on our shared moral lives.

In short, we *need* the work of analytic epistemology here to sort, and clarify, and morally highlight what so often lies unexamined as 'given' before our very eyes, even if it cannot, as such, cure us from these ills. Yet the sheer current 'normalization' of these aspects of our culture, indeed the constant reiteration of their effects, is something that bears on the sensual lives of us all, willy-nilly, and often goes in large part undetected and unanalyzed, even within religious circles (and it should be added that the available evidence suggests that religious practitioners, including clerics, are no less disposed to use pornography than the wider 'secular' public).[83] Moreover, as Lauren Winner[84] has recently argued with disturbing force and insight, religious 'practices' themselves—so much vaunted in theological discussion, since Alasdair MacIntyre's *After Virtue*,[85] as the means of the recovery of classic virtue ethics —have often themselves become means of subtly purveying and mandating sexism and racism afresh,

---

83  See again n. 76, above.

84  Lauren F. Winner, *The Dangers of Christian Practice: On Wayward Gifts, Characteristic Damage, and Sin* (New Have, CT, Yale U. P., 2018).

85  Alasdair MacIntyre, *After Virtue: A Study in Moral Theory* (Notre Dame, IN, University of Notre Dame Press, 1981).

even whilst churches simultaneously denounce such ills with apparent rhetorical fervour.

For we live, it might be said, in a culture of sensual and perceptual paradox, double-mindedness, and disassociation, where moral prurience and judgementalism go hand in hand with the veritable normalization of sensual addictions and privatized indulgence. By the same token, *Christians* of all denominations inhabit this same paradoxical world: they (we) are no less subject to the sensual blandishments of the 'hidden persuaders' than simultaneously drawn to a seemingly lost world of ascetic training of sensual and perceptual purification before God.

What, then, can we conclude from the foregoing? I come now to some tentative, but challenging, conclusions.

## CONCLUSIONS

I shall end, then, with a simple, but I hope prophetic, set of suggestions and challenges, both philosophical and theological, that take us back once more to the remarkable and neglected insights of Gregory of Nyssa on 'spiritual sensation' that we have in this lecture revisited. There is much unfinished business here, but perhaps I can at least indicate the contours of such.

First, Nyssen himself is of course in no doubt that the distortion of 'spiritual sense' is a *sin* problem all the way down, not *simply* a matter of educational opportunity, social location, 'prejudice' or differentiated political power—although all of these, we have seen, are necessarily entangled elements in the scenario of fallen sensuality. And if that is also true of contemporary racism and sexism (as I believe it to be), then theologians need to step up to the theoretic plate—as we often seem strangely unwilling to do— in seeking to clarify how sin is basic to these very same phenomena.[86] The recent philosophical trends I have just appealed to present us with enormously clarifying, indeed indispensable, *diagnoses* of what is happening in distorted perception and its many unjust and abusive outcomes; but the 'sin' narrative, I submit, is not one that can finally be bracketed out if a deeper understanding of our sensual plight is to be essayed. But nor should we simply fall back into the lazy 'liberal' assertion that 'racism *is* the original sin' (or at least 'America's original sin'), as if that just settled the matter. On the contrary, much deeper theological and spiritual work still has to be done to enunciate the precise relation, in the complex nexus of original sin, of misaligned desire, shame, 'other'-blame, self-deception, and perceptual blindness, if we are to comprehend the ongoing malaise that underlies the historic institutional forms of American racism.

---

86  This is the core project of my forthcoming *Sin, Racism and Divine Darkness* (see n. 67, above).

Secondly, what Nyssen himself sees over a life-time of reflection on the problem of a sensorium disordered by sin, is that the healing of it is precisely coterminous with the overcoming and healing of that sin, *tout court*; and thus it also takes someone a life-time—and indeed beyond, after death, according to Gregory—of longing desire, in the Spirit, to be purged, reformed and changed into the vision and life of Christ. All the practices that the Church holds out as remedies for sin are also therefore remedies, in principle, for the healing of passion and sense: our immersion in Scripture and our quest for Christ there, our participation in the sacraments, our growing in prayer and above all in contemplative practice (so that we can literally 'see' anew), and—of particular importance to Nyssen— our participation in demanding acts of mercy to the destitute in our midst. But the problem is that today these very practices seem to have failed us, or rather to have become either themselves debased from their true spiritual goals, or by degrees abandoned by us as we succumb almost unconsciously to the blandishments of those other sensual dimensions of our culture outlined earlier. In this context, then, the question of sacramental *efficacy* presses hard on us afresh, in the form of the sharpness of Gregory's ascetical test of the life-long purification of desire. It is not enough just to go through the motions and minimal requirements of the Christian round;

for life-changing sensual purgation is demanding, destabilizing, convicting, and endlessly 'stretched out in longing' (as Gregory puts it) to the *divine* goal.

Thus, thirdly and lastly, we are also struck afresh today by Nyssen's challenging and distinctive soteriological requirement that we 'work *with* the flesh to go beyond the flesh'; for the asceticism Nyssen is commending here is not that of a self-flagellating world-denial such as Nietzsche warned us of, but ultimately one of endless, desiring, growth and fructification *in the body*. We need, then, to see the 'sensual' and perceptual problems of our culture in all their complexity, richness and ambivalence, utilizing everything—to be sure—that modern philosophy can teach us in its analytic rigour; but we need also to re-draw the map of our thinking about sin and the sensual life and sanctification, and face into the challenge of how the ascetic life at its best has the capacity to change, not simply the life of an individual, but the corporate lives of churches, institutions and politics. The inner and the outer belong together—in the self, the body politic, and indeed the wider cosmos.

What would it be like, then, I ask in closing, if we were to take these very claims of Nyssen seriously now again today, and apply them—in the most practical ways of searching spiritual examination—to the deepest problems of sensation, and its tragic distortions, that our famed 'liberal' culture still immures us in? The great Jesuit reformers of the 1930s to 1960s already glimpsed in the patristic 'spiritual senses' teaching, as we saw, a nascent answer to some of the deepest theological and political challenges that faced them then. It has been the burden of this lecture to suggest that the story of 'spiritual sense' is still unfolding, and has new and profound cultural implications still to be unfurled today.[87]

---

87  I would like to thank the following for invaluable assistance during the period of researching and writing this lecture: the McDonald Agape Foundation, especially Peter McDonald, for his continuing financial and personal support; William Daniel, Martin Laird, OSA, Mark McInroy, Philip McCosker, and Philip Moller, SJ, for critical interactions and bibliographical discussions which have greatly helped the nuancing of the final text; Amanda Bourne for crucial research assistance in the era of COVID, when research libraries remained inaccessible to me; and Marcus Plested and his colleagues for the graciousness of their invitation to Marquette and their generous hospitality.

# THE PÈRE MARQUETTE LECTURES IN THEOLOGY

1969 *The Authority for Authority*
   Quentin Quesnell

1970 *Mystery and Truth*
   John Macquarrie

1971 *Doctrinal Pluralism*
   Bernard Lonergan, SJ

1972 *Infallibility*
   George A. Lindbeck

1973 *Ambiguity in Moral Choice*
   Richard A. McCormick, SJ

1974 *Church Membership as a Catholic and Ecumenical Problem*
   Avery Dulles, SJ

1975 *The Contributions of Theology to Medical Ethics*
   James Gustafson

1976 *Religious Values in an Age of Violence*
   Rabbi Marc Tannenbaum

1977 *Truth Beyond Relativism: Karl Mannheim's Sociology of Knowledge*
   Gregory Baum

1978 *A Theology of 'Uncreated Energies'*
   George A. Maloney, SJ

1980 *Method in Theology: An Organon for Our Time*
   Frederick E. Crowe, SJ

1981 *Catholics in the Promised Land of the Saints*
James Hennesey, SJ

1982 *Whose Experience Counts in Theological Reflection?*
Monika Hellwig

1983 *The Theology and Setting of Discipleship in the Gospel of Mark*
John R. Donahue, SJ

1984 *Should War Be Eliminated? Philosophical and Theological Investigations*
Stanley Hauerwas

1985 *From Vision to Legislation: From the Council to a Code of Laws*
Ladislas M. Orsy, SJ

1986 *Revelation and Violence: A Study in Contextualization*
Walter Brueggemann

1987 *Nova et Vetera: The Theology of Tradition in American Catholicism*
Gerald Fogarty

1988 *The Christian Understanding of Freedom and the History of Freedom in the Modern Era: The Meeting and Confrontation between Christianity and the Modern Era in a Postmodern Situation*
Walter Kasper

1989 *Moral Absolutes: Catholic Tradition, Current Trends, and the Truth*
William F. May

## About The Père Marquette Lecture Series

The Annual Père Marquette Lecture Series began at Marquette University in the Spring of 1969. Ideal for classroom use, library additions, or private collections, the Père Marquette Lecture Series has received international acceptance by scholars, universities, and libraries. Hardbound in blue cloth with gold stamped covers. Uniform style and price ($15 each). Some reprints with soft covers. Regular reprinting keeps all volumes available.

Ordering information:
  Marquette University Press
  Toll-Free (800) 247-6553 fax: (419) 281-6883
  Online: www.marquette.edu/mupress/

Editorial Address:
Marquette University Press
PO Box 3141
Milwaukee WI 53201-3141
phone: (414) 288-1564
web: www.marquette.edu/mupress/